D1485530

The Typhoon Story

The Typhoon Story

Tim McLelland

The
HISTORY
Press

Published in the United Kingdom in 2013 by
The History Press
The Mill · Brimscombe Port · Stroud · Gloucestershire · GL5 2QG

British Library Cataloguing in Publication Data
A catalogue record for this book is available from the British
Library.

Hardback ISBN 978-0-7524-8768-7

Typesetting and origination by The History Press
Printed in India
Manufacturing managed by Jellyfish Solutions Ltd

CONTENTS

The story of the Eurofighter Typhoon is a long and complicated saga that can be traced back to the late 1960s. It was during this period that West Germany, as it was then, first looked at possible replacement programmes for its fleet of Lockheed F-104G Starfighters. The Starfighter had already proved itself to be a very capable fighter-bomber and although West Germany had experienced many operational difficulties (largely due to its inappropriate training system), the F-104G looked set to remain in service for at least another decade. However, it was necessary to sow the seeds for an eventual replacement and this became the Neue Kampfflugzeug (NKF) programme. This was a purely national project and was not pursued with any real vigour, but it eventually re-emerged as the fundamental foundation of the Typhoon's development. Yet this search for a new fighter-bomber was far from straightforward and it would be another thirty years before the ultimate result of this aspiration would finally be achieved. What emerged was an aircraft very different to the one that might have been envisaged back in the 1960s, but it is now undoubtedly one of the most impressive and capable warplanes ever to have been created.

In the United Kingdom during the late 1960s, the Royal Air Force's air defence tasks were undertaken by numerous squadrons of Lightning interceptors, while ground attack missions were assigned to Hunters. The Harrier and Phantom were about to come into service and the Jaguar was to follow, and while West Germany was looking to the future, Britain's longer-term requirements were no more than abstract concepts. It wasn't until the 1970s that the British Aircraft Corporation (BAC, which became British Aerospace in 1977) began to look more seriously at a new fighter design: a small and inexpensive aircraft designed as a potential replacement for the hugely successful Hawker Hunter that had been exported around the world. But while the concept was being considered, it became clear that a more capable aircraft might be required for the RAF.

The emergence of America's F-16 fighter and the even more advanced F-15 Eagle emphasised how fighter-bomber capabilities were rapidly developing; and the Soviet Union's MiG-29 (and eventually the Su-27) illustrated only too clearly how the RAF's

▼ EADS Eurofighter IPA1. The 'prototype' takes to the air for the first time from Manching on 27 March 1994. (Eurofighter)

The first Development Aircraft (DA1) was meant to have the serial ZH586 in anticipation of a move to British Aerospace's Warton factory in Lancashire. However, it was retained by DASA at Manching, serial 98+29. (Eurofighter)

Did you know?
Typhoon can fly at supersonic speeds at sea level, but at altitude it can fly at more than twice the speed of sound. It also has a power-to-weight ratio of 1.15, meaning Typhoon can accelerate vertically without any aerodynamic lift.

Lightnings, Phantoms, Harriers and Jaguars would soon be outclassed by these new, high-performance warplanes. Clearly, a new tactical fighter was necessary, capable of meeting or exceeding the performance of these new-generation aircraft.

By 1977 the West German, British and French governments had come together to address this issue and consider the possibility of working together on a new programme. West Germany still needed a substitute for its F-104 Starfighter interceptors, while

◄ Germany's IPA3, pictured on a test flight with an array of laser-guided munitions, painted with high-visibility colours to aid visual and photographic tracking. (Eurofighter)

Britain and France wanted a replacement for the Jaguar ground attack aircraft which had recently entered service. Britain in particular felt that a multi-role aircraft would be a perfect solution, possibly influenced by the new F/A-18 Hornet which America was developing. In typical political fashion, a great deal of discussion took place, but it was only in Britain that any serious action was taken. British Aerospace initiated a

series of twelve Technology Demonstrator Programmes (TDPs) which would enable the foundations of a new attack fighter to be established. This move was undoubtedly bold, eventually costing British Aerospace (BAe) some £190 million, although these costs were eventually translated into huge savings when the Typhoon project eventually got under way.

▲ The DA4 loaded with FT pods and 4 x AMRAAM missiles. Based at Warton, the aircraft has been a valued part of Typhoon's test and development programme. (Eurofighter)

Jaguars, Tornados and both BAC 1-11 and Airbus test aircraft were assigned to the TDPs, exploring and developing a wide range of subjects including radar, avionics, cockpit displays, flight control systems, engines and construction techniques. Ferranti, GEC and Smiths Industries also became involved, and although the TDPs produced a huge amount of vital knowledge and data, it became clear that the different requirements and projected development time scales required by Britain, France and West Germany would make any joint programme impossible.

It was France's position which effectively blocked any further progress, as Dassault was busy producing the Mirage 2000 and the prospect of working on a joint project with Britain and West Germany was therefore of little serious interest to them. When France eventually refused to participate in any joint programme unless it was under its leadership, it became obvious that Britain and West Germany would have to abandon the concept and governmental discussions ceased in 1980.

Britain began to look more seriously at its own requirements. The RAF's Lightnings were nearing the end of their useful lives, but

➤ First flown on 8 April 2002, IPA3 has been with Germany's Operational Test Centre since August 2008. (Eurofighter)

▶ DA1 (98+29), flown by Keith Hartley, is pictured landing after a test flight at Warton in May 2006. (Chris Roche)

▶▶ Typhoon BS059 (ZK308) was decorated with an 'end of year' sticker for its first test flight, prior to being painted in air defence grey colours and delivered to the RAF. (Christian Ward)

the Phantom had assumed the air defence task after having been withdrawn from the strike/attack role. The Phantom would eventually be replaced by an interception version of the emerging Multi Role Combat Aircraft (which became the Tornado), tailored to suit the RAF's requirement for Beyond Visual Range (BVR) defence. There was no significant need for a smaller, lighter 'dogfighter' at this stage and the RAF was more interested in a suitable replacement for its Jaguars and Harriers in the attack role.

Air Staff Target (AST) 396 was created to produce what was envisaged as a Short Take Off & Landing (STOL) or Short Take Off & Vertical Landing (STOVL) aircraft, somewhat similar to the Tornado but with a single seat. This AST was eventually abandoned in favour of two separate ASTs, one of these being AST 409 for a direct replacement of the Harrier (this led to the Harrier GR5-9 series), while AST 403 was created to replace the Jaguar and the remaining RAF Germany Phantom Squadrons.

◄◄ The first flight, on 14 March 1997, of BAe's dual-control ZH590 (DA4) at Warton. Although unpainted, the aircraft sports national insignia and a multinational emblem on the nose. (Eurofighter)

◄ A magnificent image of the twin-seat DA4 leading the first and second development aircraft (DA1 and DA2) during their visit to the SBAC Farnborough Show in 2002. (Eurofighter)

DA7 on a test flight in Italy, with Alenia test pilot M. Venanzetti flying the aircraft. Operating from Caselle, it is loaded with AMRAAM and Sidewinder missiles. (Eurofighter)

BAE Systems test pilot Craig Penrice takes DA2 into the air at the 2002 SBAC Farnborough Show. (Eurofighter)

The RAF's all-important presence in West Germany required both strike/attack and fighter aircraft, therefore AST 403 was very much a multi-role requirement, returning to the earlier aims of the tri-national studies. Although primarily a ground attack aircraft, AST 403 would also require a good defensive capability that matched or bettered that of the Phantom, which it would replace. Unfettered by the complicated and expensive need for Vertical Take Off & Landing (VTOL) or STOVL (now

21

DA2 on her last flight in January 2007, en route to Coningsby where she was dismantled and transported to the RAF Museum at Hendon. ZJ804 (Typhoon T.Mk.3) was eventually delivered to No. 29 Squadron. (Tim McLelland)

only required by AST 409), the AST 403 design quickly emerged as a series of exciting and futuristic designs.

The first of these was for an aircraft which looked remarkably similar to today's Gripen, although BAe's Kingston department produced a more conventional design resembling the F-16. Meanwhile, the Warton department created an unusual model which

shared a likeness with France's Vautour from the 1960s, but with an advanced wing design and a forward fuselage like the Tornado Air Defence Variant (ADV). The various designs were undoubtedly influenced by BAe's contact with their counterparts at Messerschmitt-Bölkow-Blohm (MBB), where West Germany's future aircraft were being developed.

By this stage, West Germany's requirement for a Starfighter replacement had evolved into a more capable aircraft that could also replace the Luftwaffe's F-4F and RF-4E Phantoms, which were assigned to air defence and reconnaissance roles. Like the RAF, the Luftwaffe needed a multi-role aircraft that could function effectively as both a fighter and attack aircraft. It soon became obvious that Britain and West Germany's requirements were very similar and co-operation between the national manufacturers would make good sense.

MBB had by now established a clear preference for a delta-wing aircraft with foreplanes and either a single fin or a twin-fin arrangement as being developed on America's F/A-18. It was also adopting an under-fuselage air intake, similar to that being employed on the F-16. This was a basic design configuration that France had also considered and proposed during the early tri-national talks. But when France withdrew in favour of its own national design programmes, its concept was no longer open to scrutiny. It did, of course, re-emerge many years later as the Dassault Rafale.

The new co-operation between BAe and MBB suffered a major setback when the British government cancelled AST 403 in 1981. MBB experienced similar problems with West Germany's government and funding for Taktisches Kampfflugzeug (TKF) 90 was cut; however, the two companies

◀ ZH588 over Hampshire during the 2002 SBAC Farnborough Show. Armed with four dummy AMRAAM and two Smokewinder missiles, the all-black paint scheme was meant to disguise the 490 pressure transducers that were applied to the airframe as part of the test programme. (Eurofighter)

continued to work together on a private basis, confident that governmental interest would re-emerge.

BAe pursued what became the P.110 – a lightweight fighter design intended primarily for export. With the now familiar cranked delta wing and foreplanes (plus twin fins) the aircraft showed great promise, but without governmental support it never proceeded beyond the mock-up stage. Progress was effectively stifled without any firm interest from the government and by 1982 the Panavia companies (BAe, MBB and Aeritalia that had created the Tornado) had agreed to pursue a joint design on a private basis, in the hope that government funding would be attracted to it.

◀◀ Carrying ASRAAM and AMRAAM weapons, DA4 returns to Warton after a test flight. Brake parachutes are fitted to all Typhoons but are only used when deemed necessary, particularly on shorter runways. (Eurofighter)

◀ IPA1 (ZJ699) was assigned to release trials for the Paveway laser-guided bomb (LGB). Pictured here is a full weapons load of six LGBs, together with two ASRAAMs and a centre-line external fuel tank. (Eurofighter)

Did you know?

Typhoon was assigned to its first combat missions in 2011 when the RAF assigned the aircraft to no-fly protection patrols as part of Operation Ellamy, Britain's contribution to the UN-mandated protection of airspace over Libya. Typhoons were deployed to Gioia del Colle in Italy from where they flew combat patrols.

➤➤ IPA6 (ZJ938 – part of the RAF's Tranche 2 order) returns from a test flight at Warton during April 2008. (Mark Holt)

➤ Alenia's DA3 on its first flight, 4 June 1995. Note the Air Mobility Command chase aircraft in the distance. (Eurofighter)

The Agile Combat Aircraft (ACA) design bore a strong resemblance to West Germany's TKF 90 proposal, although it was in effect a merger of the British and German fighter-bomber designs. France remained indifferent to the programme, opting to pursue its own Avion de Combate Experimentale, which eventually became

Did you know?
Although not usually recognised as such, Typhoon is a conventional delta-wing aircraft featuring a tried-and-tested layout first pioneered by the British many decades ago. France embraced the delta-wing design for its series of Mirage fighters, but with canard foreplanes and other design improvements Typhoon's performance exceeds that of the Mirage series by a huge factor.

the Rafale. West Germany was undoubtedly frustrated that its neighbour and senior European partner would not join the ACA project, but Britain was almost relieved. Having borne the trauma of the abortive Anglo French Variable Geometry Aircraft project that France had effectively killed off, the Jaguar programme had also suffered at the hands of the French, with many potential exports lost in favour of France's Mirage F1, which France was undoubtedly keener to sell than Jaguar.

With a new tri-national project finally established, it was decided that a couple of flying technology demonstrators should be built, not only to explore and develop the technologies required for the new advanced aircraft, but to demonstrate to potential customers (not least each country's own governments) that the project would translate into an effective aircraft. One German-built and one British-built aircraft would be manufactured as part of the Experimental Aircraft Programme (EAP). A contract for the British demonstrator was signed (between BAe, Aeritalia and the

➤ ZH590 streams on to Warton's runway after completing a test flight during August 2006. (Chris Roche)

British Ministry of Defence Procurement Executive) on 26 May 1983. Unfortunately, the German demonstrator was not to follow. Before work on the British aircraft commenced, MBB announced that it was withdrawing from the project, the German government having refused to provide any funding. MBB was undeniably reluctant to pull out, but without monetary backing or any promise of eventual German interest, there was little point in remaining within the programme.

ACA was therefore dead and with it the newly contracted EAP demonstrator.

Nevertheless, BAe took a particularly bold step and opted to continue manufacturing the demonstrator as a private venture. Without the support of MBB it seemed inevitable that EAP (and therefore ACA) would be abandoned, but thanks to BAe's determination the project survived and the demonstrator was constructed as an indigenous Warton-based project, utilising components from BAe, MBB and Aeritalia, with one wing built in Italy.

In order to simplify the aircraft (thereby saving both time and money), a Tornado

Did you know?
Much of the Typhoon's structure comprises composite material, including 50% of its weight and 75% of its surface area.

rear fuselage and tail was adopted, to which the new composite aluminium, lithium and titanium structure was attached. The rear fuselage was originally meant to have incorporated new manufacturing techniques (carbon-fibre composites and superplastic-formed and diffusion-bonded titanium), but as these technologies were incorporated into other parts of the airframe, the standard light alloy Tornado rear fuselage was a much simpler alternative which merely added weight to the airframe and didn't affect the EAP's value as a technology demonstrator.

➤ Typhoon FGR.Mk.4 ZK328, resplendent in freshly applied air defence paintwork, prepares to take off from Warton for delivery to the RAF, 15 December 2011. (Mark Holt)

➤➤ The first 'diamond nine' formation of Typhoons was assembled in November 2006, with aircraft from Nos 3, 17 and 29 Squadrons, all based at Coningsby. The formation overflew the unit's home base and climbed to altitude for a series of aerial photographs. (Tim McLelland)

The ACA was to have featured twin tail fins (similar to the F/A-18 Hornet). Twin fins were deemed more suitable, as they are less susceptible to aerodynamic blanking at high angles of attack (when air flow from the fuselage and wing can mask the fin's effectiveness), and by 'toeing in' the twin rudders on take-off, the fins can increase the aircraft's rotational capability, acting as a pseudo tailplane. However, a single fin can provide space for additional fuel capacity and requires fewer mechanical

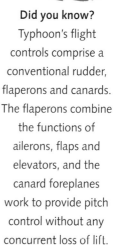

linkages and driving mechanisms, and is therefore lighter. The Tornado's large fin was judged to be more than adequate for control of lateral stability and so BAe retained this as part of the rear fuselage structure; it therefore became part of the eventual ACA (and finally Typhoon) design, almost by default.

It might be imagined that the EAP demonstrator was in essence only an aerodynamic test bed, destined to explore the capabilities of the cranked delta-wing

➤ The RAF's first nine-ship Typhoon formation, high over Lincolnshire, November 2006. (Geoffrey Lee, Planefocus/Eurofighter)

and foreplane configuration. In fact, the EAP was much more than this, and was a true technology demonstrator. Designed to be aerodynamically unstable, it employed fly-by-wire systems which had first been tested in a specially modified Jaguar. This unstable design made the aircraft extremely agile and manoeuvrable, and created an airframe with lower drag, thereby increasing speed and/or range capability. The EAP did not incorporate any weapons systems, nor did it have any radar, but it did introduce a new 'glass' cockpit layout with Multi Function Display (MFD)

As a technology demonstrator, the EAP was not a prototype of any projected combat aircraft, and on this basis the British government funded 50% of the project, clearly indicating that the financial support was not indicative of any future purchase of an operational-standard aircraft. Around 15% of the funding came from Italy, while MBB provided a token 1% in order to maintain close contact with the programme. The rest was funded by BAe themselves. Although the EAP was not a prototype for any future aircraft, its function was to test and demonstrate the technology and aerodynamics that would be put into it; it thereby influenced the design of what eventually became the Typhoon.

Apart from the adoption of a single fin, the EAP was designed as a single-seat aircraft from the outset. A twin-seat configuration could have been used, spreading the cockpit workload between the pilot and a navigator/

screens developed by Smiths Industries and a wide-angle holographic Head-Up Display (HUD) designed by GEC (originally designed for the F-16). It also incorporated a voice warning system.

weapons systems operator in the rear cockpit. This configuration had worked well for the Phantom, but Britain wanted a new fighter-bomber which incorporated a great deal of automation for routine cockpit tasks. Much emphasis was placed on the creation of a Man-Machine Interface which was both simple and intuitive, and would enable the pilot to manage the cockpit workload easily so that he could concentrate on the all-important task of aerial combat or weapons delivery. The weapons system concept and single-seat aircraft design were key aspects of the Typhoon many years later.

The EAP demonstrator (ZF534) was completed during the early summer of 1986 in No. 2 Hangar at BAe's Warton factory and comprised three major fuselage structures: front, centre and rear. The front fuselage contained many innovative structures in carbon-fibre composites and aluminium lithium alloy. The centre

and rear fuselage structures were more conventional with the modified Tornado fin being used, while the right-hand wing assembly, manufactured at the Samlesbury plant, was a co-bonded carbon-fibre composite assembly which made use of

▲ ZH590 (DA4) performed a series of air-to-air refuelling trials with RAF VC10 tanker aircraft prior to clearing the Typhoon for routine operations of this nature in RAF service. (Eurofighter)

▲ November 2007, and Eurofighter Typhoon IPA6 takes off for its first flight from Warton. (Eurofighter)

made of carbon composite at Preston and Samlesbury, and detail design and the windscreen and canopy assemblies were completed by Aerostructures Hamble Ltd on the south coast. The aircraft's first flight took place on 8 August and it quickly proved itself to be a remarkably agile and impressive machine. Fitted with a pair of RB.199 turbofans (standard power plants fitted to the Tornado) and with a considerable amount of conventional alloy structure (which made the aircraft heavier than it needed to be), ZF534 was still a sprightly performer, capable of reaching its take-off speed of 150 knots in only nine seconds. At transonic speeds the aircraft regularly left its Lightning chase aircraft behind and eventually it attained Mach 2.0 during its relatively short test programme.

new tooling and manufacturing techniques; these were put to good use later on the Eurofighter programme.

The left-hand wing assembly was manufactured at the Corso Marche facility of Alenia in Turin. The foreplanes were

Test Pilot Dave Eagles judged the demonstrator to be 'remarkably agile and very easy to fly' and believed it to be 'ideal'

and 'just what any fighter pilot would want'. He also added that he wished BAe was 'making 800 of them rather than just one'. Indeed, it is interesting to speculate whether the EAP demonstrator could have formed the basis of a new fighter aircraft without any significant further development. Certainly the aircraft had the necessary agility, and with developed engines, a direct voice system and helmet sight for the cockpit, respected author Jon Lake concluded that the RAF could

➤ IPA1 (ZJ699) is pictured during trials with the Meteor, a BVR air-to-air missile which is now standard defensive equipment for RAF, Luftwaffe, Italian and Spanish Typhoons. (Eurofighter)

➤➤ A Typhoon from RAF No. 29 Squadron poses for the camera at high altitude. This view illustrates the Typhoon's pure delta shape and the foreplane canards which provide the aircraft with outstanding manoeuvrability. (Eurofighter)

have had a fourth-generation fighter 'more than ten years before it [would] eventually introduce the definitive Eurofighter'. As it was, ZF534 completed its test programme and was retired to an engineering college in Loughborough, before finally moving to the RAF Museum at Cosford. By the time the aircraft reached the end of its useful life in May 1991, ZF534 had flown some 259 sorties.

Even though it would have been possible for BAe to develop the EAP into

Did you know?
Typhoon is fitted with a Defensive Aids Sub System in streamlined pods fitted to the aircraft's wing tips. Electronic Counter Measures (ECM) equipment is housed in the port wing fairing, while towed radar decoys are housed in the starboard pod.

▲ A close-up view of a Typhoon at Coningsby, illustrating the in-flight refuelling probe fairing, the luminescent formation-keeping strip under the cockpit, and the crew's HUD screens inside the cockpit. (Tim McLelland)

a new-generation fighter. Italy and Spain soon expressed their enthusiasm and both West Germany and France returned to discussions, having now seen the potential demonstrated by ZF534. Together, they created an Outline European Staff Target which was issued on 16 December 1983, calling for a single-seat cranked delta aircraft with canard foreplanes and a projected empty weight of 9.75 tonnes, designed for service entry in the mid-1990s. Additionally, the new multinational group initiated feasibility studies which were completed in 1984, and on 11 October that year a definitive European Staff Target was issued. Finally, a new European fighter-bomber was going ahead.

an operational fighter-bomber, Britain's government was keen to ensure that any future programme was a multinational one, both for financial and political reasons. The brave decision to 'go it alone' with the EAP demonstrator was the most important step in persuading Europe to come back on board and re-examine the possibility of

Two basic design concepts soon emerged, both of which were similar to earlier proposals (and, of course, the EAP demonstrator) but varied in important details. Although one of the designs was

Typhoon F.Mk.2 ZJ920 is high over the North Sea, proudly wearing the markings of its first RAF unit, No. 29 Squadron. The aircraft was subsequently upgraded to FGR.Mk.4 standard. (Tim McLelland)

agreed to be suitable by the four nations, France favoured a smaller and lighter design which (perhaps not surprisingly) resembled their emerging Rafale aircraft. France also continued to insist that the programme should be under France's leadership, on the basis that Dassault had experience in designing and building delta-winged aircraft. This stance ignored the fact that France's delta experience had initially been gleaned from the British, but there was undoubtedly some merit in France's

After entry into RAF service, No. 29 Squadron's Typhoons were soon embarking on exercises across the UK. Three Typhoon T1 dual-control aircraft are shown during deployment to RAF St Mawgan in Cornwall. (Tim McLelland)

assertion. Far less reasonable was France's insistence that prototype construction and all flight testing should be undertaken in France and that a 50% work share of the programme should be theirs. In effect, France was proposing a French aircraft built for French requirements, but funded by other countries. One commentator remarked that he wondered 'what France would have demanded had it not been interested in collaboration and had wanted to put us off the idea'!

It was clear that France's participation would not only be impractical, but utterly

poisonous to the whole programme. It was at this stage that France finally left the project for good, even though there was a short-lived suggestion by the United States that a true NATO-wide enterprise could be developed to encourage co-operation between European countries and the US.

However, the idea went no further and France went off to pursue Rafale, while the remaining countries (Britain, West Germany, Spain and Italy) moved towards Project Definition during June 1985.

On 1 August the countries agreed to proceed with the established design, which

➤ Typhoon T1 from No. 29 Squadron gets airborne. It is fitted with a robust landing gear which, although sturdy, is not designed to give the aircraft a 'rough field' capability. The air intake doors are fully open as the aircraft climbs under full power. (Tim McLelland)

was essentially a direct development of the EAP.

Work share was agreed with 38% for Britain, 38% for West Germany, and 24% for Italy, changed to 33, 33 and 21% in September so that Spain could come on board with a 13% share. Almost comically, France continued to express interest in the programme, even offering at one stage to settle for design leadership and a 31% work share. By this stage the foundations of a combat aircraft programme had been set and France's ludicrous attitude was ignored.

The participating nations eventually fixed on a common design which catered for the needs of each country. The RAF's requirements had shifted slightly since the project was first considered: there was still a need to replace the Jaguar squadrons based in West Germany and the UK, but there was also a pressing urgency to release the air defence Phantoms based in West Germany. Although the Tornado ADV was destined to replace both the Phantom and Lightning in the UK air defence role, the Tornado was a long-range interceptor designed to operate in the BVR role, launching 'fire and forget' missiles against incoming targets. In contract, the Phantoms in West Germany were tasked with the air defence of a much more local region and needed more effective close-in defence capability both in terms of weapons and manoeuvrability. In essence, this meant a classic dogfighter, but the RAF was keen to ensure the new aircraft could handle the Jaguar's ground attack tasks and be capable of operating from improvised sites such as motorways and cleared fields.

The RAF stipulated that the new aircraft should be capable of operating from a 500m (1,640ft) landing strip. This contrasted with some of the requirements set by the other participating countries. Italy needed to replace its Starfighters (an aircraft that certainly didn't have any short field capability), primarily in the air defence role, while Spain was interested in a multi-role aircraft with a good ground attack capability. West Germany was looking for a Phantom replacement, having substituted its Starfighter attack squadrons with Tornado Interdictor Strike (IDS) aircraft. This meant an agile fighter with a secondary reconnaissance capability.

These combined requirements could be seen as contradictory, but the basic aim of creating a multi-role aircraft meant that the fighter and attack roles could be handled by one generic design. By December 1985 a European Staff Requirement for a European Fighter Aircraft (EFA) was issued and a Project Definition study was completed by September the following year. The study revealed some potential difficulties, not least that the aircraft would have to be bigger and heavier than envisaged. The RAF's requirements dictated that the aircraft needed an empty weight of around 11 tonnes in order to provide the necessary weapons load and range capability. This was not popular, as a heavy aircraft was less exportable, and the RAF eventually

Did you know?
Like the aircraft, Typhoon's engines are the result of multinational co-operation. Designed and built by Eurojet, the consortium embraces Rolls-Royce, Motoren-und Turbinen-Union (MTU), Fiat Avio and Industria de Turbo Propulsores. The EJ200 engine will continue to be improved and developed.

➤ Three Typhoon T1 aircraft share RAF St Mawgan's huge apron with a single Typhoon F2. All four aircraft are from No. 29 Squadron, based at Coningsby. (Tim McLelland)

relaxed its requirements and settled on a common design.

There were many other disagreements, too, such as West Germany's insistence that the American AN/APG-65 radar should be used and that General Electric engines should be installed in the initial pre-production aircraft rather than the RB.199, which was being developed specifically. There was also much debate over the work share figures, and whether these should be proportionally based on projected orders for each country, or based on the need for avionics commonality. There were negotiations with Belgium, who expressed a desire to join the programme in August 1986, but these came to nothing; it was perhaps not surprising that France's interest re-emerged, the suggestion being made that its Rafale and the new EFA could share a variety of common avionics and equipment items. This idea was soon abandoned.

The project continued, but it was not an easy progression. Eurofighter Jagdflugzeug GmbH was created to manage the joint programme, but West German politicians became increasingly reluctant to allow the EFA programme to continue unchecked. West Germany's defence minister, Manfred Woerner, called for a DM2 billion reduction in the EFA research and development costs,

◄ This underside view of a Typhoon F2 manoeuvring illustrates the wing's extended leading edge slats (vital for low-speed handling), chaff/flare dispensers and missile troughs under the fuselage. (Tim McLelland)

based on his projections of West Germany's financial status and military capabilities. MBB endeavoured to co-operate but Woerner began to study alternatives to the EFA, including a notionally cheaper Hornet derivative and an advanced F-16, but neither aircraft offered the same capability and any significant reduction in cost.

Once again, Britain tried to kick start the floundering programme and confirmed its commitment to EFA's full-scale development

had slowly matured to incorporate the large, square-shaped intakes under the fuselage, and the removal of the radar warning receiver fairings on the fin. The empty weight had now been fixed at 9.75 tonnes (a further 250kg allocated to national equipment fits), although ironically this was revised upwards to incorporate convergent-divergent exhaust nozzles that were stipulated by West Germany in order to improve supersonic performance.

West Germany's requirements caused many other headaches and delays. Perhaps the most serious was its clear preference for American radar. The Luftwaffe wanted the AN/APG-65, much to the surprise of Britain, who assumed that West Germany would adopt a pro-European stance. Perversely, West Germany was loudly criticising Britain for allowing an American company to effectively take over Westland Helicopters (instead of adopting a European

phase on 25 April 1988, in the hope that the other nations would do the same. A Memorandum of Understanding was signed by Britain, West Germany and Italy on 16 May, and was endorsed by Spain in November. The Full Scale Development contract was finally signed on 23 November 1988, based on the approved design which

case of self-interest – their F-4 Phantoms were, of course, fitted with American radar.

The advantage of European radar soon proved hard to resist, and it became clear that the adoption of American radar would result in restrictions on potential exports, thanks to the constraints placed on technology transfer by the US. In any case, the choice of radar was non-negotiable as far as Britain was concerned. Apart from replacing RAF Germany's Phantoms, the new EFA would be assigned to UK air defence and would require a good BVR capability – something that the American radar didn't possess.

The EFA's engines were another source of contention. It seemed logical to adopt the RB.199 turbofan to power the pre-production EFA aircraft (and the first twenty production machines), chiefly because Britain, West Germany and Italy were

solution) while at the same time advocating the use of American radar in the new EFA, even though an all-European radar would have been more effective and a better deal for European manufacturing. West Germany's reasoning was that the American radar could be introduced far more swiftly than an all-new European solution, but in reality West Germany's preference for American radar was simply a

A pilot's eye view of a typical scene at RAF Coningsby as Typhoons from Nos 29 and 3 Squadrons return from a training mission. The lead aircraft is breaking to port to join the downwind leg of the airfield circuit. (Eurofighter)

already familiar with the engine, which powered the Tornado IDS and ADVs in service with these nations. The new Rolls-Royce EJ200 projected for the EFA offered great potential, and it seemed logical that it could be retrofitted to the Tornado fleet as part of update programmes, if required. But for reasons that have never been made clear, West Germany proposed the use of the General Electric F404, even though

Spain was the only participating country that used this engine and had nevertheless accepted that RB.199 was a better solution. Eventually, West Germany accepted the view of the other three nations and RB.199 was finally adopted to power the first EFAs, with installation commonality with the EJ200 so that this engine could be retrofitted at a later stage.

Even more difficult was the establishment of work share between the participating countries, with many decisions being based on rigid percentage agreements or simple political considerations. The most

No. 17(R) Squadron is the RAF's Tornado Operational Evaluation Unit (OEU) responsible for the integration of the aircraft into operational service. ZJ912 was one of the first Typhoons to operate with this unit and is pictured landing at its home base at Coningsby. (Tim McLelland)

➤ A typical scene at Coningsby, with a No. 29 Squadron Typhoon returning from a training flight. With the Cold War now over, RAF bases have abandoned camouflage for airfield support vehicles, and despite the Typhoon's drab grey paintwork, its home base is surprisingly colourful. (Tim McLelland)

troublesome of these issues was the development of the EFA's Flight Control System (FCS). BAe was given leadership of the avionics integration programme and it was therefore inevitable that the FCS development would be awarded to Germany's Daimler-Chrysler Aerospace AG (DASA). DASA did have some experience on this front, having operated the F-104CCV aircraft – a neutrally stable machine designed to explore digital fly-by-wire control systems. However, when compared to BAe and GEC, DASA's background knowledge was limited: the ACT/FBW Jaguar had demonstrated a far more relevant quadruplex fly-by-wire system that was almost ideal for the EFA. Of course, Britain had also designed, built and operated the EAP demonstrator, so it appeared obvious that GEC should handle the task. GEC also claimed it could design the EFA's FCS for one-third of the cost projected by DASA. Eventually, both BAe and GEC took over the EFA's FCS after DASA proved to be incapable of solving various software problems. Eurofighter explained this shift in work share allocation as a response to a reduction in German orders, but it was arguably the logical solution that should have been adopted in the first place.

▲ The RAF's Typhoon units have all adopted their own individual markings which have been applied to a standard format on Typhoons. Oddly, the unit markings are applied in full colour, while the aircraft's national insignia are still presented in low-visibility pink and lilac colours. (Eurofighter)

Construction of the first EFA began in 1989 and in May 1992 the prototype was transferred from DASA's Ottobrunn facility to Manching, where it made the first installed engine runs on 6 June. The programme then suffered further delays, largely because of the FCS software problems, but also due to German politics. Having signed the Maastricht Treaty, Germany was obliged to maintain tight fiscal control in order to establish monetary union with the rest of Europe, and having already become severely strained by the reunification with East Germany, it was inevitable that the Eurofighter (as it soon became known) would become a political Aunt Sally. Portrayed by German politicians as a relic of the Cold War, there was easy political advantage to be made by openly opposing the EFA. Matters reached almost absurd proportions when, for example, the

chief executive of the State of Brandenburg (sponsors of the ILA 1992 Air Show) refused to attend the event simply because a Eurofighter mock-up was on show.

The situation reached crisis proportions in the summer of 1992 after Germany announced withdrawal from the project.

▶ Typhoons high over Lincolnshire. The aircraft in the foreground carries the markings of No. 29 Squadron, a former Phantom unit. The lead aircraft are from No. 3 Squadron, a former Harrier unit which joined No. 29 Squadron at Coningsby after relinquishing its Harriers at Cottesmore. (Geoffrey Lee, Planefocus/ Eurofighter)

British Prime Minister John Major went to Germany to talk with Chancellor Kohl, who agreed to continue supporting development but did not make any commitment to financing production. Having originally agreed to purchase 250 aircraft (which were in many ways designed to Germany's requirements), the projected purchase was now 80 aircraft – a figure which the Luftwaffe regarded as unviable. This impasse prompted Germany, Italy and Spain to look at alternative aircraft, and although there was no obvious change in Britain's position, it seems likely that a potential purchase of either the F-15 or F/A-18 was examined.

Germany eventually concluded that the EFA was by far the least expensive and most effective solution, but this was a bitter pill to swallow for many German politicians, who began to refer to Eurofighter as 'Das Englische Flugzeug' (The English Aeroplane). One could argue that this was totally at

odds with reality, as the EFA was geared as much towards German requirements as Britain's, and all four participating nations accepted that the EFA was the most suitable aircraft even though – by its very nature – it was a compromise solution.

German pressure ultimately resulted in the EFA becoming a more austere machine.

▲ A Typhoon from No. 11 Squadron, one of four Typhoon units based at Coningsby, gets airborne. Typhoon units have now formed at Leuchars (Nos 1 and 6 Squadrons), but as this base in now scheduled for closure the Typhoons may eventually transfer to Lossiemouth. (Eurofighter)

Renamed Eurofighter 2000, the aircraft was presented as a baseline airframe that customers could elect to equip with high-cost systems depending on what was required or what could be afforded. Some reports suggest that the aircraft's short field capability was relaxed somewhat, but in essence there was little that could be done to make any substantial reductions to the aircraft's overall cost. It was expensive, but it represented better value for money than any competing programme. Meanwhile, Italy maintained a stoic position, even though they had the most urgent need for the Eurofighter.

Italy's fleet of F-104G/S Starfighters was undoubtedly obsolete. Magnificent though this aircraft was, it had to be replaced. One commentator described the F-104 as a 'treasured vintage Ferrari' that Italian pilots occasionally took out for a drive on the *autostrada*. Italy concluded that it

Did you know?

Typhoon has an impressive short field take-off and landing capability. A lightly loaded Typhoon can reach its take-off speed of around 110 knots in five seconds. With the aid of its braking parachute, landings can also be remarkably short if necessary.

could not wait for the Eurofighter and an interim solution was found in the shape of a fleet of RAF Tornado F3 interceptors, which were supplied to Italy on a lease basis, agreed in November 1993. Spain remained patient, while Britain continued to push for progress, and when the ongoing FCS problems were finally solved, the first prototype (DA1) made its maiden flight from Manching on 27 March 1994, a staggering two years later than planned. Despite the investment of so much British expertise and support, the first flight was conducted from a German airfield using an aircraft sporting German markings, and flown by a German test pilot (Peter Weger).

➤ Luftwaffe single-seat Eurofighters over Lithuania during a deployment in support of NATO's policing of the Baltic States. From Fighter Wing 74, the aircraft are carrying IRIS-T missiles and centre line-mounted external fuel tanks. (Geoffrey Lee, Planefocus/Eurofighter)

➤➤ High over Lithuania during a patrol mission, a pair of Typhoons from Fighter Wing 74 pose for the camera. In addition to the centre line external tank, only a pair of IRIS-T missiles is carried by each aircraft. (Geoffrey Lee, Planefocus/Eurofighter)

There were many observers who begrudged the fact that Germany was seemingly being rewarded for its reluctant participation in the programme; however, others believed that a perceived German leadership was a small price to pay if it ensured Germany stayed with the programme.

DA1's first flight was a great success. Accompanied by an Alpha Jet and Phantom chase aircraft, the aircraft (serial 98+29) climbed to 10,000ft and attained 300 knots, and although the first flight was a low-key affair, DA1 was soon attaining 450 knots and altitudes of up to 36,000ft, performing manoeuvres up to 5g. Over in England, the second prototype (DA2) was prepared for flight at Warton and, after delays caused by poor weather, Chris Yeo took ZH588 on a fifty-minute flight on 6 April. It seems likely that weather wasn't the only cause of ZH588's hold-up: the recent loss of Lockheed's YF-22 and Saab's JAS39 Gripen was sufficient to cause a great deal of worry within Eurofighter. Although confident in the EFA's FCS, Warton's team

In RAF service, the Meteor air-to-air missile will replace the AIM-120 Advanced Medium Range Air-to-Air Missile (AMRAAM) as Typhoon's primary defensive weapon by 2015. An extremely capable BVR weapon, Meteor is likely to become a primary defensive weapon with other Typhoon operators as well.

➤ An alternative view of a Typhoon from Fighter Wing 74 at Neuburg. The pilot's work space inside the Typhoon is fairly small but comfortable, with an array of CRTs immediately ahead of him and a HUD. All-round visibility is excellent. (Geoffrey Lee, Planefocus/Eurofighter)

may have thoroughly checked and double-checked the FCS before allowing ZH588 to get airborne.

DA1 and DA2 proceeded to complete fifteen hours of test flying each before being temporarily grounded. There was speculation that the programme had encountered serious technical problems but the aircraft were simply being refitted with more developed avionics and an improved FCS. The real delays were caused by Germany's continual reluctance to support the venture fully. Funding was slow and often insufficient and Germany continued to insist that it retained a 30% work share, even though it was now proposing to buy 25% of the planned production. Its expectation that it should be prime contractor for production was illogical. Even more ludicrous was the proposal to merge Eurofighter with Panavia, under the leadership of a German managing director. But stoic acceptance of Germany's position continued and even though its attitude contributed to increased costs, the increasingly austere aircraft that Germany wanted was ultimately little different to that ordered by Britain, Italy and Spain.

The adoption of the title Eurofighter 2000 for the EFA did little to change the direction of the programme, which stalled while Germany's politicians wrestled with the issue. Britain insisted that further slippage in production would be 'unacceptable', but this did little to push Germany into action. Likewise, Britain's unilateral agreement to begin production in September 1996 achieved nothing. By the beginning of 1997 the situation was as bleak as ever, and Germany's politicians attempted to stall progress still further when it became clear that Britain would soon be ruled by a new Labour government, which, based on its historical dislike for military spending, might abandon the Eurofighter, thereby enabling Germany to neatly escape from the programme by default. Remarkably, the shadow defence secretary informed Germany that despite plans for defence cuts, Eurofighter would be excluded from

Did you know?
Typhoon is manufactured in six main sections. The forward fuselage (built by BAe) is married to a centre section (built by DASA), while the rear fuselage is manufactured by both CASA and Alenia. The starboard wing is made by CASA and BAe, while the port wing is built by Alenia. Components are then completed in final assembly facilities in each country.

➤ A pair of Typhoons from Fighter Wing 74 prepares to embark on a training mission from Neuburg. Although wearing typical grey camouflage (of a slightly different shade to that applied to RAF aircraft), the Luftwaffe continues to apply full-colour national insignia and serials to its aircraft. (Geoffrey Lee, Planefocus/Eurofighter)

➤➤ The Typhoon's cockpit is typical of any modern warplane. With a simple and uncluttered layout, the main instrument panel is dominated by three MFD units and a HUD. (Eurofighter)

this process and Britain would procure the planned 232 aircraft under the new government. This news came as something of a blow to many German politicians and, with no other obvious way forward,

Germany signed a production investment Memorandum of Understanding.

The third development aircraft (DA3) made its first flight on 4 June 1995. This aircraft (MM-X-602) was completed and flown from Alenia's Caselle airfield, flown by test pilot Napoleone Bragnolo. Fitted with initial standard EJ200 engines, the aircraft acquired production standard engines by the end of 1997. The new engines were satisfactory and their performance was as good as, or better than, expected. On one early test flight DA3's pilot accelerated to supersonic speed at 40,000ft, at which stage the engine afterburners were deselected. Much to the pilot's surprise, DA3 continued to accelerate in 'dry' (un-reheated) power.

Just two months after DA3's initial flight, the first dual-control EFA took to the air from Spain's Getafe facility, on 31 August. The twin-seat trainer version of the EFA was an important part of the programme from the outset, with all four participating nations anticipating a dual-control variant which could be used for conversion and continuation training. Designed as a minimal-change version of the standard

airframe, the twin-seater is slightly heavier than its single-seat counterpart and carries slightly less internal fuel (despite an additional fuel tank in the enlarged dorsal spine), but it maintains the same performance characteristics. Although the dual-control variant will be allocated to training duties, it will inevitably be used in an operational role if necessary and it seems likely that specialised versions of the

◄◄ Fighter Wing 73, a combined training and operational air defence unit, received its first Typhoons in April 2004. One of the unit's first aircraft was 30+42, which is shown here during winter operations at Rostock-Laage. (Geoffrey Lee, Planefocus/ Eurofighter)

◄ A wintry scene at Rostock as a Typhoon from Fighter Wing 73 roars into the air, trailed by a cloud of snow. (Geoffrey Lee, Planefocus/Eurofighter)

twin-seater may well emerge in the future, designed for specific missions.

The first production contract was signed on 30 January 1998 between Eurofighter GmbH, Eurojet (a consortium comprising Rolls-Royce, Germany's MTU Aero Engines, Spain's Industria de Turbo Propulsores and Italy's Avio) and NETMA (the four-nation customer organisation). The procurement totals were set as follows: UK – 232;

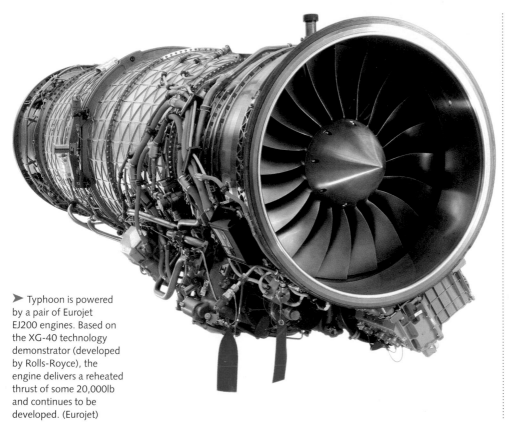

➤ Typhoon is powered by a pair of Eurojet EJ200 engines. Based on the XG-40 technology demonstrator (developed by Rolls-Royce), the engine delivers a reheated thrust of some 20,000lb and continues to be developed. (Eurojet)

Did you know?
Britain's Development Aircraft DA1 (98+29) first flew in 1994. It is now grounded and on display at the RAF Museum at Hendon, having made its last flight to Coningsby, from where it was transported to London by road.

➤ The Typhoon incorporates an arrestor hook which is used only for emergency landings. The brake parachute is housed between the jet pipes and is used for routine landings on shorter runways. The arrestor hook provides a safety back-up should the parachute fail. (Eurofighter)

▲ Looking deep into the EJ200 engine exhaust, the complicated structure illustrates the high-tech nature of the engine's design, resulting in a small and lightweight engine that delivers high thrust. The exhaust features a typical convergent/divergent nozzle design. (Eurojet)

Germany – 180; Italy – 121; and Spain – 87. Production was again allotted according to projected procurement: British Aerospace – 37.42%; DASA – 29.03%; Aeritalia – 19.52%; and CASA – 14.03%.

In September 1998 the EFA enjoyed a particularly high profile at the Society of British Aerospace Companies (SBAC) Farnborough show. During the event the

aircraft was relieved of its unwieldy and unimaginative name and a more appropriate title for any projected export aircraft was bestowed upon it – Typhoon. A great deal of thought had gone into the naming process, as the tastes of four nations can be very different. There was significant British enthusiasm for naming the aircraft Spitfire II, but with Germany as a major partner in the programme this would have been less than tactful. Finding a name which translated into each country's language wasn't easy, but eventually 'Typhoon' was accepted as a good compromise, having been applicable to a less-than-successful

◄ RAF Coningsby's Eurojet EJ200 maintenance facility. A gleaming EJ200 receives attention from RAF personnel, and the convergent/divergent nozzles are clearly visible. (Eurofighter)

RAF fighter-bomber but also to the German Bf 108 Taifun decades previously. It was proposed that all export versions would be referred to as Typhoons, but when the first aircraft were delivered to the RAF they swiftly adopted the name; although Germany, Italy and Spain claimed their aircraft would still be known as EFAs or Eurofighters, the name Typhoon has now been adopted by each country.

73

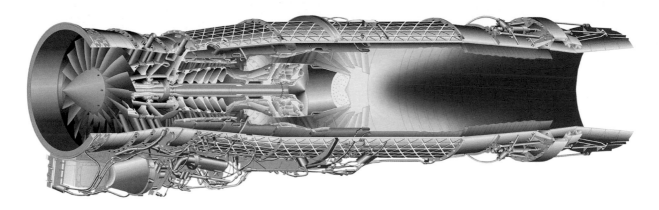

▲ Although complex in design, the basic function of the EJ200 is remarkably simple and little different to a typical turbojet/ turbofan design found in countless combat aircraft. (Eurojet)

Further Development Aircraft soon joined the programme, the last of the initial seven aircraft being (thanks to a change in the delivery schedule) the British DA4, the second twin-seater aircraft to be completed, which took to the air on 14 March 1997. The first Instrumented Production Aircraft (IPA) were next to emerge, with IPA2 making its first flight from Turin on 5 April 2002. Just a few days later IPA3 made its maiden flight from Manching and finally, on 15 April, IPA1 got airborne from Warton. After a long and sometimes precarious journey, the Typhoon was ready to enter service.

Final German approval to purchase the Typhoon came in October 1997 and the first series production aircraft for Germany took to the air on 13 February 2003; this was the first of 180 aircraft destined to join the Luftwaffe to replace the F-4 Phantoms and

The first Typhoons for No. 6 Squadron arrive at RAF Leuchars in Scotland, September 2010. The unit's well-known markings have already been applied, the famous 'flying can opener' motif visible on the aircraft's tails. (Eurofighter)

MiG-29s, and to replace partially some of the service's Tornado aircraft. As with so much of the Typhoon programme, Germany was seen to be leading the way, and so it was the next day that the first British (BT001) and Italian (IT001) aircraft made their first flights, followed by Spain's ST001 three days later. On 30 June Type Acceptance was signed to mark the formal delivery of the first aircraft to each of the Eurofighter nations.

The RAF established its first Typhoon unit on 1 September 2002 when the Typhoon OEU was created at BAE Systems' (formerly BAe) Warton factory. This unit was responsible for evaluating the new aircraft, examining its capabilities and looking at how to integrate it into regular squadron service. The OEU moved to Coningsby on 1 April 2005 and became No. 17(R) Squadron, tasked particularly

with evaluating the Typhoon's weapons capabilities and tactical use. Formal activation of this first Typhoon squadron at RAF Coningsby occurred on 1 July 2005. No. 29(R) Squadron then re-formed as the Typhoon Operational Conversion Unit (OCU), directed to train the RAF's Typhoon aircrew. The first regular squadron to equip with the Typhoon was No. 3 Squadron, having exchanged its Harriers for Typhoons

➤ A Typhoon from No. 11 Squadron RAF launches a Paveway 2 laser-guided bomb. The weapon's fins have deployed and the bomb is about to be directed towards its target by the Litening Target Designator Pod also being carried by the aircraft. (Geoffrey Lee, Planefocus/Eurofighter)

and re-forming at Coningsby on 31 March 2006. The Typhoon then progressively replaced the RAF's Tornado F3 fleet and took over responsibility for UK QRA on 29 June 2007, becoming formally declared as an advanced air defence platform on 1 January 2008.

Initial production aircraft of the Tranche 1 standard (Typhoon F.Mk.2) were capable of air-to-air roles only and were the first Typhoons to hold UK QRA duties. In order to deploy RAF's Typhoons to Operation Herrick (Britain's deployment to Afghanistan), urgent single-nation work was conducted on the Tranche 1 fleet to develop Typhoon's air-to-ground capability in 2008. Tranche 1 aircraft were thus declared as multi-role in July 2008, gaining the designation FGR.Mk.4 (the twin-seat variant re-designated as the T.Mk.3), fielding the Litening Laser Designator Pod (LDP) and Paveway 2, Enhanced Paveway 2 (laser-guided bombs) and 1,000lb free-fall class of weapons. Only a handful of F.Mk.2 and T.Mk.1 aircraft still remain in RAF service, and these will be upgraded to the FGR.Mk.4 and T.Mk.3 standard probably by the end of 2013.

Tranche 2 aircraft (the second batch of British aircraft) deliveries commenced under the four-nation contract in 2008, and were all completed to perform the air-to-air role

◄ A No. 3 Squadron Typhoon on exercise over Dubai. Visible here, just ahead of the wind shield, is the Passive Infra-Red Tracking Equipment – Infra-Red Search and Track (PIRATE IRST) fitted to RAF Typhoons. PIRATE performs the same function as radar but in a passive mode. (K. Tokunaga/Eurofighter)

➤ ZJ932 prepares to depart on a mission from Coningsby. The port wing tip pod housing ECM radar-jamming equipment is visible. The black staining on the centre fuselage is caused by the aircraft's Auxiliary Power Unit (APU) exhaust. (Tim McLelland)

➤➤ No. 6 Squadron on Exercise Bersama Lima in Malaysia in 2011. RAF Typhoon pilots operated alongside Royal Australian Air Force F/A-18 pilots, Malaysian MiG-29s and Singapore's F-15 and F-16s; they also gained the opportunity to train in tropical conditions. (Geoffrey Lee, Planefocus/Eurofighter)

only. Some of these aircraft were deployed to the Falkland Islands in September 2009 to take over air defence duties from the Tornado F3s based there, and the Tranche 2 fleet continues to be slowly brought up to a common standard with full air-to-ground capability. A total of fifty-three Tranche 1 aircraft were delivered to the RAF, with a Tranche 2 contract provisioning for ninety-one aircraft. Some twenty-four of these were diverted to Saudi Arabia in order to meet an urgent export requirement, leaving

➤ Exercise Bersama Lima saw four Typhoon FGR.Mk.4s deploy to the Royal Malaysian Air Force base at Butterworth. The 7,000-mile trip involved stops in Jordan, Oman and Sri Lanka. (Geoffrey Lee, Planefocus/Eurofighter)

sixty-seven due for delivery to the RAF. The Tranche 3 contract has been signed and this will deliver a further forty aircraft. It then seems likely that the early Tranche 1 aircraft fleet will be retired over the period around 2018, and this will leave 107 Typhoon aircraft in RAF service until the currently projected withdrawal date in 2030.

Germany's Luftwaffe began taking deliveries of Typhoons in May 2004

 A No. 3 Squadron RAF Typhoon fires an MBDA ASRAAM missile against a flare pack towed by a Mirach target drone at the Aberporth range in Cardigan Bay, Wales. The pilot is Flt Lt B. Cooper. (Eurofighter)

when Fighter Wing (Jagdgeschwader) 73 re-equipped with the aircraft at Rostock-Laage. Fighter Wing 74, at Neuburg an der Donau, followed in July 2006. The first Typhoons assigned to the air-to-ground role were delivered to Jagdbombergeschwader 31 at Nörvenich towards the end of 2009, becoming operational the following June after replacing its fleet of Tornados. Equipped with free-fall and laser-guided bombs, the

> Exercise Bersama Lima marked the fortieth anniversary of the Five Power Defence Arrangements between the UK, Malaysia, Singapore, Australia and New Zealand. No. 6 Squadron successfully completed more than seventy sorties during the detachment, amounting to 164 flying hours. (Geoffrey Lee, Planefocus/Eurofighter)

unit is now operational with the GBU-48 LGB and Designator Pod. Two more Luftwaffe units are also re-equipping with the Typhoon, these being JG 71 at Wittmund and JGB 33 at Büchel, which is expected to take its final deliveries by 2015. Like the RAF, the Luftwaffe assigned Typhoon to QRA duties and by the summer of 2008 it had taken over responsibility for this interception role from the ageing F-4F Phantom.

In Italy, the first operational standard Typhoon was handed over on 20 February 2004 at Cameri. On 16 March, 4° Stormo/9 Gruppo took delivery of IT002 (twin-seater), the first single-seater arriving in January the following year. The unit was declared operational on Typhoon twelve months later, by which stage Italy too had committed the Typhoon to QRA interceptor responsibility, allowing the much-loved F-104 Starfighter (and an interim fleet of F-16s which had been leased as a follow-on from the batch of Tornado F3s which were returned to the RAF) to be completely withdrawn from Italian service. The 36th Wing at Gioia del Colle was the next unit to re-equip, together with the Italian OCU 20 Gruppo at Grosseto.

In Spain, meanwhile, four units (plus an OCU) are re-equipping with Typhoons. Unusually, the Typhoon is designated as the C.16 in Spanish service (the twin-seaters being CE.16), although as with all other nations, the aircraft will probably be referred to by air and ground crews as the Typhoon. No. 113 Escuadrón was formed at Morón in January 2004 as the Typhoon OCU, and Nos 111 and 112 Escuadrones became the first two operational units (also based at Morón) and both are expected to be declared fully operational by 2015. Nos 141 and 142

▲ A close-up view of 30+21. Luftwaffe Typhoons are not equipped with the RAF's PIRATE system. The port canard foreplane is visible, as are the smaller strakes fitted under the cockpit canopy. These smooth out vortices generated by the foreplanes. (Eurofighter)

➤ A member of Fighter Wing 74's ground crew prepares an IRIS-T air-to-air missile for flight, prior to a training sortie from Neuburg. (Eurofighter)

Escuadrones will also re-equip with the type, possibly at Albacete. The first delivery to Spain (ST001) arrived on 5 September 2003, with the first single-seater arriving in December 2004; by July 2008 Spain had allocated Typhoons to operational QRA air defence duties.

The Typhoon is also enjoying some export success, although overseas sales have not been as plentiful as Eurofighter

◀ A line-up of three Typhoon tails at Gioia del Colle. The tail markings are those of No. 12 Squadron, the second front-line Italian air force Typhoon squadron to form. (Geoffrey Lee, Planefocus/Eurofighter)

might have hoped for. Austria opted to purchase the aircraft in July 2002 as a new fighter destined to replace a fleet of aged Drakens. Eighteen aircraft were agreed on, although by June 2007 this order had been reduced to fifteen. The first delivery was made on 12 July 2007 and the Typhoon has now settled into operational service, but not without controversy. Allegations persist that political lobbying influenced Austria's

A No. 12 Squadron Typhoon at Gioia del Colle is refuelled. Ease of maintenance was a key element of the design process, ensuring that the Typhoon is reliable and, therefore, relatively inexpensive to operate. (Eurofighter)

A pair of Typhoons from Italy's 4° Stormo/ 9 Gruppo during a patrol mission from Grosseto. Italian Typhoons from this unit were tasked with the air defence of the region around Turin during the Winter Olympic Games in 2006. (Eurofighter)

order and that sums of up to $100 million used to support this lobbying have tainted what was Eurofighter's first export order.

Equally controversial was the sale of seventy-two Typhoons to Saudi Arabia, the order (placed in August 2006) having been won after a fierce battle with France who was keen to sell them the Rafale. Continuing allegations in the UK over the Al-Yamamah arms deal (secured in the

1980s) undoubtedly hindered negotiations between the Eurofighter nations and Saudi Arabia, but eventually twenty-four aircraft were agreed on (the first handover taking place on 11 June 2009), these being diverted from the production order for the RAF. A further forty-eight aircraft will be assembled in Saudi Arabia.

Efforts to sell the Typhoon to India failed after a long and intensive campaign that was ultimately thwarted by France, and a lower bid for a fleet of Rafales. Likewise,

Italy's Typhoons are equipped with the PIRATE search and track system. The first Typhoon to be delivered with PIRATE was to the Italian air force in August 2007. (Eurofighter)

attempts to export the Typhoon to Japan looked promising until US pressure to buy the F-35 (on the basis of its better stealth characteristics) led to the abandonment of this sales campaign. Other orders seem likely, but uncertain. Greece certainly has a requirement for the Typhoon, but with a crippled economy it is probable that an already-obsolete fleet of F-4 Phantoms and A-7 Corsairs will remain in use for some time. Qatar is also considering a Typhoon order and other countries may eventually emerge. Among the most likely are Denmark, Norway, Romania, Switzerland and Turkey.

It would be fair to say that the Typhoon suffered from a long and precarious gestation period. For many years it seemed likely that the Eurofighter concept would never be translated into reality, and when more concrete plans were finally made to produce the new combat aircraft, it became a political football which rarely received the financial backing it required. But despite this troubled history, the Typhoon has emerged as an outstanding warplane. The programme did suffer setbacks thanks to a variety of technical glitches, but most of the Eurofighter's delays were caused by politics. By 1998 the British National Audit Office had estimated Typhoon's unit cost at £40.2 million per aircraft. If development costs are added into the equation, each Typhoon cost £61 million. This is an astonishing figure for a small fighter aircraft, but when compared to its counterparts it is in fact a surprisingly competitive one.

The Dassault Rafale can be calculated at costing £72 million per aircraft, for a design that is somewhat less capable than the Typhoon. The sophisticated F-22 Raptor weighs in at a staggering £122 million per aircraft, and although models such as the F-15 and F/A-18, plus the F-16 and even the MiG-29, can be regarded as competitors in terms of overall cost, they don't match the capabilities of the Typhoon. It can be concluded, therefore, that the Typhoon represents excellent value for money. However, it could also be stated that the programme could have been completed more economically had politics not intervened.

The creation of a single final assembly line and a single flight test centre would undoubtedly have saved a great deal of

◀ A pilot's eye view from inside a Luftwaffe Fighter Wing 74 Typhoon as aerial refuelling takes place. All typhoons are equipped with extendable refuelling probes, enabling the aircraft's range and endurance to be extended as necessary. (GAF/Eurofighter)

money. As it was, the utilisation of four was wasteful, but necessary in order to satisfy the political demands of each participating nation. This made the programme artificially expensive, but it was a price that each nation was prepared to pay in order to achieve a political aim. Nevertheless, the act of creating a multinational programme did result in a very capable warplane that would have been far more expensive to design and manufacture had the project been tackled by just one country.

Another important point to consider is that the projected costs which will be incurred throughout the Typhoon's life span were factored into the design. Low maintenance and reliability were key design aims and Eurofighter ensured that in terms of potential technical problems, the Typhoon would be able to rectify at least 50% of any such defects within forty-five minutes and 95% within three hours. It was also stipulated that each engine could, if necessary, be replaced within forty-five minutes and that overall ease of maintenance was catered for. The Typhoon, therefore, is a remarkably reliable machine that can be maintained with relative ease – in stark contrast to many older combat aircraft that were sometimes regarded as logistical nightmares (the Lightning, for example). It will be cheaper to operate than its counterparts and its reliability means that fewer aircraft need to be maintained in operational condition at any given time.

The most important issue to consider is whether the Typhoon delivers everything that was expected of it. Initial speculation suggested it was not as manoeuvrable as its potential adversaries (the Su-29 and MiG-29 in particular). This was nonsense, and it was probably the first public demonstrations of the Typhoon that led to such premature conclusions. Eurofighter deliberately kept Typhoon's display flights within

◀◀ A No. 3 Squadron Typhoon over Dubai during an overseas exercise and air show appearance. (K. Tokunaga/Eurofighter)

conservative limits during the programme's early days in order to avoid stretching the known performance envelope ahead of the development process. This encouraged uninformed observers to conclude that Typhoon was not an agile 'turn and burn' dogfighter, but nothing could have been further from the truth. The Typhoon is more than capable of engaging in combat with its contemporaries and adversaries. It can out-turn all of its competitors and above supersonic speeds it can outmanoeuvre the Su-27 and MiG-29. At high subsonic speeds only the F-22 and thrust-vectoring Su-27 can offer a better sustained turn rate and, of course, it is unlikely that Typhoon will ever be required to engage either of these aircraft in combat. It could be argued that Typhoon is a superior aircraft to every other comparable type, other than the somewhat over-specified (and monstrously expensive) F-22.

The Typhoon doesn't have thrust vectoring, and it is unlikely it ever will, but the capability is there and much research and development has been conducted on potential thrust-vectoring systems. The aircraft's rear bulkhead is capable of being retrofitted and if a suitable engine derivative is produced, only new software would be required to enable the Typhoon to embrace thrust vectoring. The Typhoon could also be utilised as a seaborne multi-role aircraft and various studies have been

Did you know?
Although the Typhoon is not designed for stealth, it has a very low frontal radar signature that enables the aircraft to press home an intercept without being easily detected by radar.

◄◄ A pair of Austrian air force Typhoons on a mission from Zeltweg. Austria's Typhoons are not equipped with the nose-mounted PIRATE system. (Eurofighter)

➤ This impressive nose-on view of two Austrian Typhoons illustrates the flattened upper fuselage ahead of the engine exhausts and the prominent fuselage strakes fitted above and behind the canard foreplanes. (Markus Zinner/Eurofighter)

completed that suggest it could easily be modified for carrier operations. The sorry tale of Britain's new carrier programme often included the possibility of modifying some British Typhoons to operate at sea, and this would have been a more logical and less expensive solution than the F-35 order that is currently being pursued. But once again, it seems that politics have prevailed over common sense.

Did you know?

Typhoon is fitted with a Martin Baker Mk.16A ejection seat. It can operate up to an altitude of 50,000ft and is capable of safely ejecting from zero altitude and zero speed. Special flying clothing provides pressurised anti-g protection and enables the Typhoon pilot to tolerate up to 1g more than his counterparts.

◀ The first export aircraft for Germany (AS001) made its first flight from Manching on 21 March 2007. Aircraft 7L-WA, shown here, was the first aircraft to be delivered to Austria, arriving at Zeltweg on 12 July 2007. (Eurofighter)

▶ Factory-fresh paint glistening, two Austrian Typhoons pose for the camera. Aircraft 7L-WD first flew on 27 November 2007, while 7L-WE made its first flight slightly earlier on 8 November. The former aircraft was delivered to Austria on 21 December 2007 and the latter on 15 April 2008. (Eurofighter)

▶▶ Two new Typhoons embark on a post-delivery flight after joining the Austrian air force. Their pristine condition is compromised only by the sorry stains around the aircraft's APU exhaust. Even the EJ200 engine convergent/divergent nozzles are still brilliantly clean. (Eurofighter)

Another much-discussed issue is the Typhoon's stealth capabilities. When compared to the impressive F-22 it is clear that Typhoon is not a true 'stealth' aircraft. However, it is important to consider Typhoon's multi-role capabilities and the scenarios in which it is expected to operate. Designed as an agile interceptor-fighter, it only really needs a low radar signature from a head-on aspect, as most fighter

◄ A classic aerial image, mirroring an iconic photograph taken by the late Arthur Gibson many decades ago, of two RAF Lightnings. With afterburners ignited, these two Austrian aircraft break left and right for the cameraman. (Eurofighter)

Did you know?

Typhoons in RAF service operate both from conventional concrete aprons and from Hardened Aircraft Shelter (HAS) complexes. Unlike with the Tornado and Phantom, the RAF's HAS can accommodate two Typhoons if necessary thanks to the aircraft's relatively small size. However, many of the RAF's Typhoons now operate from conventional flight lines, the need for HAS accommodation having reduced since the end of the Cold War.

Eurofighter Typhoon

Navalised Typhoon

1. Localised structural strengthening
2. Localised Engine strengthening
3. Modified Arrestor Hook
4. Strengthened larger stroke undercarriage
5. Thrust Vectored Engines

engagements begin from a head-to-head position, particularly in the all-important BVR scenario that is the Typhoon's key role. Typhoon's rather ungainly square intakes certainly don't give the impression that stealth technology has been incorporated

➤ Single- and twin-seat Typhoons from Ala 11/ Esc 13 on a training flight from their base at Morón. Spanish aircraft are officially referred to as the C.16 Tifon. (Eurofighter)

▶ From March 2011 the RAF deployed Typhoons to Gioia del Colle in Italy as part of NATO's response to the Libyan crisis. Typhoon ZJ927 from No. 3 Squadron proudly wears a tally of LGB mission launch markings. (Eurofighter)

Did you know?

Although fitted with conventional engines, Spain has been leading the development of a thrust-vectoring system for Typhoon. A fully functional vectored thrust nozzle has been designed and continues to be developed; it may be fitted to some Typhoons in the future, but current Typhoon operators have not expressed any significant interest in the concept.

An impressive close-up look at a Typhoon from No. 3 Squadron over Libya, with refuelling probe extended, LGBs ready for launch, and AMRAAMs under the fuselage. Two LGB mission marks are applied under the cockpit. (Eurofighter)

◄ Typhoon tails in the heat of a Spanish sunset. These aircraft are from Ala 11/Esc 13 based at Morón. (Eurofighter)

C.16-22

C.16-26

C.16-33

Did you know?

Typhoon's performance figures are impressive with a top speed of Mach 2.0 and a maximum range of 2,350 miles (although combat radius figures are, of course, much lower). Its rate of climb is 62,000ft per minute and with a maximum altitude ceiling of 65,000ft, Typhoon can reach this height in little over a minute.

into them, but first impressions can be deceptive. Throughout the Typhoon's development and initial operational use, a great deal of care has been taken to prevent photographers capturing clear images of the Typhoon's internal air intake design structure. The intake does incorporate some carefully designed curves which shield

the engine compressor blades from radar detection and it is likely that the intake is stealthier than it first appears.

The Typhoon was subjected to a great deal of Radar Cross Section (RCS) testing, much of which was observed on a special range at BAE Systems' Warton site. Eurofighter admit that all-aspect stealth capability was never an aspiration (it would have been too expensive), but they claim that only the F-22 has a lower frontal RCS. They maintain that Typhoon's frontal RCS is probably one-seventh of the Su-27's and one-fifth of the F/A-18 Hornet's. Even the elegant design of the Rafale doesn't compare well, with Typhoon's frontal RCS being one-third of the Rafale's. This is quite an achievement, although there is always the possibility that Eurofighter's overt RCS testing and the quirky restrictions on intake photography might be an elaborate bluff to compensate for a RCS that isn't as

◀◀ Cassadian's 300th Spanish-built Typhoon is suitably decorated to celebrate the achievement. The aircraft was subsequently delivered to Ala 11/Esc 13 at Morón. (Eurofighter)

◄ Saudi Arabia is purchasing seventy-two Typhoons, the first twenty-four of which were manufactured at BAE Systems' Warton factory. The remaining aircraft for the order will be assembled in Saudi Arabia from components supplied by the Eurofighter consortium. (Eurofighter)

▼ One of an initial batch of aircraft for the Saudi Arabian air force, pictured landing at Warton after completing a shake-down test flight prior to delivery to the RSAF. (Christian Ward)

القوات الجوية الملكية السعودية
ROYAL SAUDI AIR FORCE

ZK073

٣٠٥
305

good as Eurofighter claim. What is certain, however, is that the Typhoon is an agile and manoeuvrable aircraft that is able to carry a varied and weighty ordnance load. It is also capable of 'supercruise' performance, whereby the aircraft maintains supersonic speed without the use of engine reheat (afterburners). This means the Typhoon does not necessarily have to accelerate into a missile interception, and it can enter and escape hostile zones much more swiftly (and economically) than its counterparts. During test flights the Typhoon was routinely observed to lose speed when reheat was deselected at speeds of Mach 1.4 or more, but the aircraft settles into supercruise without reheat at around Mach 1.1 and can sustain this speed as required.

Although the Typhoon is now firmly established in operational service with the RAF, Luftwaffe and the air forces of Italy, Spain, Austria and Saudi Arabia, it is inevitable that the aircraft will become part of other air forces too, and that it will be developed still further, both to increase its already impressive capabilities and to enable it to take on new tasks. Its weapons capabilities will be continually improved, ensuring that the Typhoon continues to be a potent warplane for at least another two decades. Its troubled development programme was unnecessarily

Did you know?

The introduction of Typhoon into operational service will continue for some years, particularly with the RAF. No. 1 Squadron re-formed on the type late in 2012 and at least one more RAF squadron will receive Typhoon when final deliveries of new-build aircraft are completed.

◄◄ Sunset at RAF Coningsby in Lincolnshire, as the last Typhoon mission of the day comes to an end and the roar of the mighty Typhoon ceases – until another day. (Tim McLelland)

long and complicated, but the participating Eurofighter nations can be justifiably proud of the magnificent warplane that emerged. Britain (and BAE Systems) can be particularly proud of the support and investment that was put into Eurofighter – often at times when other countries were all too keen to walk away. Britain's persistence and belief in the aircraft resulted in what is arguably the most capable fighter-bomber ever to have served with the RAF.

Many of Britain and Europe's combat aircraft designs have suffered from political indecision, lack of finance, design requirement shifts and all manner of problems which compromise the capabilities of the final product. It might have seemed inevitable that a complicated four-nation European aircraft would suffer more than most. But even though the project had its difficulties, it is clear that – for once – the result was an outstanding machine that has not been compromised in any way by its complex development and history. The Eurofighter Typhoon – by any standard – is a magnificent success.

Jan 1994   Germany, Italy, Spain and the United Kingdom agree on a revised European Common Staff Requirement for development of a new European fighter aircraft

Mar 1994   Prototype Eurofighter DA1 makes its first flight from Manching in Germany

Apr 1994   Second Eurofighter (DA2) makes its first flight from Warton

Jun 1995   Third Eurofighter (DA3) makes its first flight from Caselle in Italy

Jan 1996   Revised work share arrangements for aircraft production are agreed between the four participating nations

Aug 1996   First twin-seat dual-control Eurofighter (DA6) makes its first flight from Seville in Spain

Feb 1997   Fifth aircraft (DA5) makes its first flight from Manching – the first aircraft to be equipped with the newly developed Captor radar

Mar 1997	Second twin-seat aircraft (DA4) equipped with Captor radar makes its first flight from Warton
Jul 1997	DA2 deploys to RAF Leeming to undergo hardened shelter compatibility trials
Oct 1997	500th test flight is achieved at Manching
Dec 1997	Eurofighter flies with large external stores; the first test firing of a Sidewinder AIM-9L and AIM-120 AMRAAM missile; Eurofighter's first flight at Mach 2.0
Jan 1998	Production and Support contracts for 620 Eurofighter aircraft are signed for the participating nations; Eurofighter's first in-flight refuelling with RAF VC10 tanker
May 1998	First metal is cut for production aircraft at the European Aeronautic Defence & Space Company (EADS) Augsburg facility in Germany

Jun 1998	Eurofighter Development Aircraft fleet completes its 750th flight and reaches 630 flying hours; DA4 undergoes lightning strike trials at Warton; the Royal Norwegian Air Force evaluates Eurofighter DA5 at Rygge
Jul 1998	DA6 goes to Morón Air Force Base in Spain for extreme temperature trials
Oct 1998	Supplement 2 to umbrella contract is signed in Munich for production of first tranche of 148 aircraft, together with long lead items for Tranche 2; the fleet achieves its 800th flight; the name 'Typhoon' is adopted for the export market
Nov 1998	Test fleet passes 700 flying hours
Dec 1998	Fleet achieves its 900th sortie; work begins on sub-assemblies for the first production aircraft at Samlesbury and at EADS in Bremen
Jan 1999	First parts for the first right wing of production aircraft are machined at EADS in Spain

Feb 1999	Assembly of the first centre fuselage sections starts at EADS at Augsburg; Greece announces its intention to procure sixty to eighty aircraft; DA3 flies for the first time with wet fuel tanks, testing the functionality of the fuel system; Eurofighter receives a proposal from Norway for twenty aircraft, plus an option for a further ten
Mar 1999	DA3 flies supersonic with external fuel tanks
Apr 1999	Greece confirms intention to join Eurofighter programme, leading to an order for up to ninety aircraft
May 1999	DA5 flies the test fleet's 1,000th sortie
Jun 1999	Eurofighter receives Requests for Information from Netherlands, Czech Republic and Poland, together with a Request for Proposal from the Republic of Korea for forty to sixty aircraft
Dec 1999	Eurofighter's first flight at Mach 1.6 with 3 x 1,000l external tanks

Jan 2000	DA6 undergoes icing trials in the environmental hangar at Boscombe Down
Feb 2000	1,000th flight test hour is achieved, flown by DA4 from Warton; DA5 participates in flight icing tests behind a Dornier icing tanker
Mar 2000	Greek parliament announces its intention to procure sixty Eurofighter Typhoons, plus an option for a further thirty
May 2000	DA4 completes the first twin-seater night flight from Warton
Jun 2000	BAE Systems (formerly BAe) opens Eurofighter final assembly hangar at Warton
Jul 2000	DA1 and DA2 perform at Farnborough Air Show – the first time two Typhoons have flown together in public
Sep 2000	Final assembly of the first production Eurofighter Typhoon begins at Warton

Apr 2001	DA7 undertakes weapon test trials at Decimomannu, including the successful launch of AIM-9L and AMRAAM
Jun 2001	Further weapon trials launch with advanced short range air-to-air missiles (ASRAAM) at Decimomannu by DA7
Jul 2001	First flight with outboard store station fitted and equipped
Aug 2001	First in-flight refuelling from a Tornado, equipped with a buddy-buddy pod
Nov 2001	AMRAAM jettison trials at Mach 1.6; the first flare-firing trials
Jan 2002	Crew escape system tested at 600kt on a ground sledge
Mar 2002	Radar AMRAAM firing clearance achieved
Apr 2002	First flight of IPA2, from Turin; first flight of IPA3, from Manching; first flight of IPA1, from Warton
Jul 2002	Austrian government begin negotiations for the procurement of up to twenty-four Typhoons

Nov 2002	Loss of DA6 in Spain due to an engine failure
Feb 2003	First four Series Production Aircraft (SPA) make their maiden flights in each participating country
Jun 2003	Type Acceptance signature is achieved, allowing the delivery process for Typhoon to commence
Aug 2003	First production aircraft (GT003) is delivered for instructor training at Manching
Oct 2003	First Spanish Eurofighter is handed over to Wing 11, the first Eurofighter squadron to be formed in Spain; integration trials for the Meteor BVR air-to-air missile begin at Warton
Dec 2003	4° Stormo, Italian air force, receives its first Typhoon
Feb 2004	IPA4 makes its first flight – the first single-seat production aircraft
Apr 2004	First series of in-flight gun firing trials of the BK 27 Mauser cannon and the first air launch of an IRIS-T SRAAM are completed

May 2004	First German air force Typhoons are delivered to Fighter Wing (Jagdgeschwader) 73 at Rostock-Laage
Oct 2004	First flight of GS002, the first single-seat series production Typhoon
Nov 2004	Eurofighter Typhoon IPA2 completes the first night air-to-air refuelling test
Dec 2004	Signature of the Tranche 2 Supplement 3 contract, allowing for the production of Tranche 2 Eurofighter Typhoons that feature full air-to-air and air-to-ground swing-role capability
Jun 2005	More than fifty aircraft now in service with the four partner air forces, following simultaneous acceptances by the German and Spanish air forces; Eurojet delivers the 250th SPA EJ200 engine
Jul 2005	RAF's No. 29(R) Squadron moves to RAF Coningsby, from Warton
Nov 2005	Italian air force surpasses 1,000 operational flying hours, and the entire in-service fleet achieves 5,000 flying hours. Major General Klaus

L. Axelsen, chief of the Royal Danish Air Force Air Materiel Command, takes a VIP back-seat flight in Typhoon; on landing, he states: 'You should be proud of this very capable aircraft'

Dec 2005   UK signs agreement with Saudi Arabia for a Typhoon order; final flight of DA1 after eleven years of flight operations

Feb 2006   Italian air force deploys two Typhoons from 4° Stormo to patrol the skies over Turin during Winter Olympics – the first time a partner air forces uses the aircraft operationally

Mar 2006   No. 3 (Fighter) Squadron of the RAF at Coningsby becomes the first operational RAF Typhoon squadron

May 2006   IPA4 becomes the first Typhoon to carry out air-to-ground weapon release

Aug 2006   Typhoon in-service fleets surpass 10,000 flying hours

Oct 2006	First Tranche 2 Typhoons begin final assembly in Germany and UK; delivery of 100th SPA (BS022) to RAF; four-nation flight test fleet achieves 5,000th Typhoon flight
Nov 2006	Retrofit R2 programme begins, in which all earlier capability standards in Tranche 1 (Block 1, 2 and 2B) are brought up to the Final Operational Capability Block 5 standard
Dec 2006	First flight of a Block 5 SPA (SS011) completed at Morón in Spain
Feb 2007	Type Acceptance of the Block 5 standard aircraft is completed: Block 5 aircraft provide full air-to-air and initial air-to-ground capabilities
Mar 2007	AS001, for the Austrian air force, makes its first flight
May 2007	The four partner air forces achieve 20,000 combined flight hours
Jun 2007	Eurofighter and Austria reach agreement on cost reductions and a reduced order for fifteen aircraft; RAF assigns two Typhoons to twenty-four-hour QRA duties at RAF Coningsby

Jul 2007	AS001 is delivered to Austrian air force
Nov 2007	First flight of IPA6, the first Typhoon to be loaded with Tranche 2 avionics, at Warton; first LGB drop using a Litening III LDP at the Aberporth Weapons Range
Dec 2007	Eurofighter GmbH sign contracts for the supply of seventy-two Typhoons to Saudi Arabia
Jun 2008	Completion of Typhoon's first annual Exercise Green Flag at Nellis Air Force Base, USA; Fighter Wing 74 starts NATO QRA duties with Typhoon
Oct 2008	Spain takes delivery of a Tranche 2 aircraft (SS012); first aircraft for Saudi Arabia makes its maiden flight; BS040 delivered to RAF, marking the beginning of Tranche 2 aircraft deliveries to the four partner air forces
Nov 2008	Eurofighter test fleet surpasses 6,000 flying hours
Dec 2008	Combined Typhoon fleets in Germany, Italy, Spain, UK and Austria achieve 50,000 flying hours

Jan 2009	12 Gruppo at Gioia del Colle in Italy begins QRA air defence duties
Jun 2009	First two Typhoons delivered to Saudi Arabian air force
Sep 2009	Fifteenth and last Typhoon for Austria delivered
Feb 2010	Spanish air force Typhoon fleet reaches 10,000 flying hours
Jan 2011	Operational fleet of Typhoons in service reach 100,000 flying hours
Mar 2011	Typhoon begins combat missions in Libya as part of Operation Odyssey Dawn: RAF's Typhoons provide ground attack capability as British forces support NATO operations in Libya; Typhoons carry Enhanced Paveway 2 bombs for the operation
Jun 2011	300th Typhoon produced is delivered to Spanish air force, making Typhoon the only new-generation multi-role aircraft to reach the impressive figure of 300 examples in service

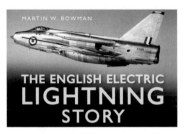